Michelangelo's Seizure

Michelangelo's SEIZURE

Poems by Steve Gehrke

University of Illinois Press

Urbana and Chicago

Library of Congress Cataloging-in-Publication Data
Gehrke, Steve.
Michelangelo's seizure / Steve Gehrke.
p.   cm. — (The national poetry series)
Contents: Self portrait as the head of Goliath —
Self portrait with doctors — Monet going blind —
At the anatomy lesson of Dr. Tulp —
Renoir, arthritic — Michelangelo's seizure —
Late self portrait — The death of the Virgin —
Magritte in New York — Self Portrait as St. Sebastian
pierced by arrows — [etc.]
ISBN-13: 978-0-252-03169-4 (cloth : alk. paper)
ISBN-10: 0-252-03169-5 (cloth : alk. paper)
ISBN-13: 978-0-252-07420-2 (pbk. : alk. paper)
ISBN-10: 0-252-07420-3 (pbk. : alk. paper)
I. Title.
PS3557.E3549M53   2007
811'.6—dc22   2006029377

The National Poetry Series

The National Poetry Series was established in 1978 to ensure the publication of five poetry books annually through participating publishers. Publication is funded by the late James A. Michener, the Copernicus Society of America, Edward J. Piszek, the Lannan Foundation, the National Endowment for the Arts, and the Tiny Tiger Foundation.

2005 Competition Winners

Steve Gehrke of Columbia, Missouri, *Michelangelo's Seizure*
Chosen by T. R. Hummer; published by the University of Illinois Press

Nadine Meyer of Columbia, Missouri, *The Anatomy Theater*
Chosen by John Koethe; published by HarperCollins

Patricia Smith of Tarrytown, New York, *Teahouse of the Almighty*
Chosen by Edward Sanders; published by Coffee House Press

S. A. Stepanek of West Chicago, Illinois, *Three, Breathing*
Chosen by Mary Ruefle; published by Verse Press/Wave Books

Tryfon Tolides of Farmington, Connecticut, *An Almost Pure Empty Walking*
Chosen by Mary Karr; published by Penguin Books

Acknowledgments

AGNI: "Late Self-Portrait," "Vanitas for Robert Mapplethorpe"
Green Mountains Review: "Jackson Pollock Driving"
Iowa Review: "Magritte in New York"
Kenyon Review: "The Anatomy Lesson of Dr. Tulp"
Marlboro Review: "Self-Portrait as the Head of Goliath"
Michigan Quarterly Review: "Gassed"
North American Review: "Renoir, Arthritic"
Ontario Review: "The Burning of Parliament, 1834"
Prairie Schooner: "Self-Portrait with Cataracts"
Pushcart Prize XXXI: "Gassed"
Shenandoah: "The Death of Sardanapalus"; "The Machine Gunner's
    Letters" (part II, as "from the Machine Gunner's Letters")
Southern Review: "Remembering Camille" (as "Monet Going Blind")
Southwest Review: "Francis Bacon in His Studio"
Threepenny Review: "Double Elegy, 1918"
Virginia Quarterly Review: "Goya at the Madhouse," "Michelangelo's
    Seizure," "Self-Portrait with Doctor"
Washington Square: "The Death of Pointillism"
Yale Review: "The Raft of the Medusa"

"Self-Portrait as the Head of Goliath" won the *Marlboro Review* Poetry
    Prize and the Milton Dorfman Poetry Prize.
"The Burning of Parliament, 1834" won the William Faulkner–
    William Wisdom Poetry Prize sponsored by the Pirate's Alley
    Faulkner Society.
"The Death of Pointillism" won the *Washington Square* Poetry Prize.

Thanks to Jason Koo, Sherod Santos, Lynne McMahon, Phil Pardi,
Jessica Garrett, and Nadine Sabra Meyer.

For Nadine Meyer,
absolutely

. . . that gaze which is not merely a messenger of the eyes, but at whose window all the senses gather and lean out, petrified and anxious, a gaze eager to reach, touch, capture, bear off in triumph the body at which it is aimed, and the soul with the body.

—Marcel Proust

Contents

Self-Portrait as the Head of Goliath

When, in Naples, estranged
from his paternal Rome,
Caravaggio dreamed the boy
he killed back onto the tip
of his blade, his sword bending
again under the boy's sudden weight,
he worked all night, with oils
and dread, and self-love, which is the eye
at the center of our grief, altering
the lines of the lips, darkening each hair
on the beard, and swirling his gaze
into the giant's eyes, until his own face
bloomed like an exiled flower
from the stalk of Goliath's neck,
loose veins dangling like roots, and when
he had finished, two brushes drying
on a windowsill, the city
blushing with an early dawn
below, he could hear
the sellers' carts being wheeled
into the marketplace, he could sense
himself, each painted atom,
in a mound of fruit spilled into the street,
the arc of his life, for the first time
in months, cast out beyond his fear,
so that he knew there might be
some small portion
of pleasure, even in the dying,
some sweetness. Then,
because the murderer inherits

the sins of the murdered one,
or because of exile and arrogance,
all those miles to Rome, like the stations
of the cross, because of anxiety,
or the fruit sellers, outside, calling forth,
greedily, their own portions
of the day, the most famous
painter on earth felt his death
warrant flutter like a flag above the Rome
inside of him, and when he turned
back to the painting, when he stared
into the spotlight of his face, his head swinging
in David's hand, like a lantern,
as if it might guide them, fearless,
through the valley of their myth,
he felt the self evaporate,
the way a reflection is absorbed
into a stained-glass window,
so that he could pray not for pardon
or forgiveness, but for the boy he killed
to be called forth into the frame,
into David's face, made tender
by the slaying, resurrection light
all along his skin, so that he
could ask with humility,
and for more than himself: *of sins,*
are all our paintings made?

Part I

Self-Portrait with Doctor

After Goya

Heat-struck, bleached, a sucked pit
rolling in the mouth of his fever, he lies there,
   ready for the leech,
     anxious, brave, his soul stamping
in the bull-ring of consciousness,
   but fragile too, a blown-glass stomach,
       the bones in his wrists like chalice
stems, the first leech soft upon his skin,
        like a brush-tip,
      like a tongue, the doctor probing,
       trying to look inside, scooping
his arms around him from behind,
    so that Goya dreams
he's a soldier
    being dragged from the front,
      the beautiful Spanish dust kicked up
  into his eyes, the doctor dropping a lantern
      into the sinkhole of his lungs, urging him
to cough the bullets of infection
    out, though when Goya feels the rim
of the water-glass flush against his lips,
    it's as if the reared-back horses change
      to marble in his gaze, rifles
losing their erections,
    bullets leaving only clothes-lines
     in their paths, so that he's hiding
     himself away again, smuggled in the basket
   of laundry his mother carries
     through the yard, wobbling, trying not
      to let her see, the wind
     fluttering the shirt-tail of his hair,

his body
        turned now to equal parts tenderness
                and rage, the crossed swords
of his ribcage being raised
                even as the doctor prepares
        to dunk him in the washing tub again,
            using his forearm like a blindfold
to protect the eyes, though,
        at once, Goya glimpses
            his own face,
                a watery self-portrait
        that wrinkles through his mind—
which is how I saw him that morning,
        more than a dozen years ago, strung between
my draining tubes as the machine churned
            the blood out of me,
        his face fleeting but complete,
            flapping like the tail of a deer,
a streak of white that I followed
        through the green forest light of a seizure.

Monet Going Blind

Work of the eyes is done, now
Go and do heart-work
On all the images imprisoned within
 —RILKE

1. Remembering Camille

It's like the art of making a woman
   blush from across
the room, that kind of looking—
   hollowing, aggressive—
but internalized now, so that even
   as he feels the light
glinting off the buttons of his coat,
   as he hears the light
playing his buttons like a flute,
   the avalanche
of his beard teased into a fine mist,
   as if at any moment
he might begin to float, he can't help
   but think that he is merely
old, the watery self flowing
   always inward now. He holds
the brush, not like a baton
   to the music of the shore,
not like a scalpel or a key,
   not the way a mother holds
a spoon to the child's mouth,
   but almost, yes, like an arrow
he's withdrawing, with experience
   and love, from the chest
of a dying man, so as to let the wound
   bleed out, the way,

years earlier, when he'd looked
    deep enough, into church-
stone, or the impossibly intricate mind
    of the haystack, he'd
slowly remove the injection of the gaze,
    he'd begin to reel
the gaze in, so that the jeweled
    secrets, the hard pitted light
at the quietness of objects, would leak
    into the air, would haunt
the exterior—a membrane, a mirage.
    It's blinding, he thought,
the pace with which the mind
    converts light into more
than itself, that holy photosynthesis,
    into field dust and mood,
into memory, the infinity of twigs,
    linseed upon the grindstone,
bits of oil paint splattered in
    the snow, like colored bird-
droppings, his wife once
    joked. And when she lay
dying, the doctor saying his good-byes,
    Monet, knowing he shouldn't,
stood before her, already mixing
    the colors, a drip-cloth
unrolled across the carpet,
    three-legged easel
locked in place. Awash in a torrent
    of blankets, she lay
all night for him, a reluctant muse, drifting
    through the insomnia
of lanterns, as he swayed at the edge
    of her bed, almost fatherly,

but doing something
    she couldn't quite name,
not quite a blessing or a spell,
    but trying to lure
something out of her, something
    she wanted, all at once,
desperately to keep, until there
    was a sweetness
in the air, something she could
    have sworn was a mist
of her perfume. At Giverny,
    standing on the platform
he had made, with brush cup
    and easel built in, pulleys
anchored to the bridge,
    Monet remembers her
as he lowers himself
    through the wind,
as he walks out everywhere
    on the diminishing
tightrope of his sight. Her whole life,
    he thinks, packed,
with the landscape, into memory's
    foolish mothball light.
Below him, the lilies,
    shifting and tethered,
appear as footprints across the water,
    the tracks perception
leaves, though all motion
    is exterior to them,
a display of current, of wind.
    Once, with his second wife,
in Venice, a pigeon landed
    on the tips of his fingers,

then disappeared into his sleeve.
    A moment of panic,
the coat shucked off in flurry,
    the pigeon loosed,
and his first wife floating towards
    the ceiling again, as he stood
there shivering, the coat
    lying rumpled at his feet.

2. Self-Portrait with Cataracts

It's appalling, the way the light escapes.
—MONET

Because art gives our own loss
    back to us, camouflaged
as beauty, because the self,
    distilled, echoes back
through harbor stone and lily,
    through rose-arch
and wisteria, he paints, finally,
    himself retreating
into the foxholes of his eyes,
    his whole face smudged
beneath the cataract's gleam,
    drowning in the broth light,
one eye covered completely
    when he paints,
the other made planetary
    in the atmospheric glass,
his monocle, gold-rimmed,
    radiating scowl-lines
around the eye, so that when
    he places the canvas
on the floor as if to look
    upon a landscape,
he sees, among the white-tipped
    reeds and the bridge
frowning across the wrinkles
    of the face, two birds
where the eyes had been,
    their feathers tucked in,
heads bowed, not moving at all,
    though their feet paddle

desperately beneath. Hovering
   like that—ethereal,
not a self, but a wave
   curled up out of the self,
so its reflection is its source—he feels
   a storm break inside
his face as a light mist rises
   from the paint, the way,
years earlier, the ground floor
   abandoned to the flood,
he stood, upstairs, watching torn
   leaves smeared across
the water, violent and seductive,
   like the trail of clothes
across a bedroom floor, although—
   he remembers remembering
this—it was February, so that he
   was watching, not leaves,
but the ruins of his own uprooted
   garden, a flotilla
of marguerites and bellflower,
   processional of blue
thistle, pink sumac, Alice,
   behind him, shivering
in the bed, feverish, leukemia
   passing through her,
poisonous as color through a leaf,
   the hook of each breath
unstitching something inside,
   as if she were becoming
the rattle in the shutters,
   as if she were slowly turning
herself into the window
   he was gazing through,
so that he knew, even then,
   that he would never

not be looking through her,
    each morning, in the mirror,
his face laid on top of her face.
    When she died, he prayed,
one night, for whatever comes
    to lean down over him
and pluck the flowers of his sight.
    Going blind, he imagined,
was a way to feel her
    leaving him again, as his first
wife had, his whole life now
    like a fist loosening from
around the moment of his birth.
    But the hand keeps
longing for the weight
    of the amputated brush,
and his hand would unfurl
    each stroke from the memory
of tendons, of light, as now,
    leaning down
to darken out the eyes,
    he remembers, at the window
again that night, seeing,
    on the surface, like a tiny
lighthouse tumbled from
    the shore, the lantern
he had hung one morning
    in a tree, still lit, the severed
branch holding it up above
    the waves. And how later,
when she grew silent, he held
    a small mirror just above
her mouth, then swiped, almost
    thoughtlessly, a finger
through the breath
    he'd captured on the glass.

At the Anatomy Lesson of Dr. Tulp

The split body is taboo, must not be looked
upon—not even by the doctor, vacant beneath
the charcoal of his hat, his hands working

on their own, one cleaving the muscles open
for the light, all sexed leaves and petal-swarm,
sheared away from the trellis of the bones,

the other hand mirroring the motions these muscles
would permit, which is where the students look,
trying to see the cadaver's reflection in the doctor's

skin, like Perseus capturing Medusa in his shield,
as if one glimpse of the dead man's soul might
turn their coppery faces into stone. Audacious,

self-adoring, a devil's tail of hair silking down
his back, Rembrandt will not be distracted,
not by the book-light texting the body, not

by the dumb-show of the doctor's hand,
not by the muscles in his own arm which constrict
and separate as he paints, preparing to flatten

the body, make it into color, shades of light,
perspective, what the soul might be if he could
capture it, like a moth trapped in an upturned glass,

the suffocating wing-flutter arrested on his brush,
though it's his own soul he unearths, of course,
the cadaver's skin turning slowly into the frozen,

winter-light of memory, the plagued and anemic
village of his childhood, all ice-floe and broken
arteries, a mud-horse breaking an ankle in the slush,

reared back, the death-cart toppled in its wake,
the dull-eyed, naked bodies spilling through the artist's
mind, the death-flies, the stench. Is this what I have

to wade through, he thinks, the sloppy intestines
of these streets, art like a rag pressed against
a gagging mouth, a way to hold the horror back?

It's almost paralyzing now, the stillness of the corpse's
face, the sprung bowels, the wet and marbled muscles
turned over in the light, then the sound of something tearing,

and a darkness revealed in him, death in the upturned
soil of the heart, venomous, swift, so terrifying
that it must be taken in with a shadow-glance and peak,

like a poison downed in sips, like the one scene
I can't quite imagine from my life, corpse-like beneath
the surgery lights, the doctors masked, slowly breaking

into me, like outlaws gathered around a safe, the tissue-
spreaders, the clamps, the dead man's kidney coiled
atop the surgeon's hand, already polluted, the infection

hidden, like a flame at the center of coal, a piece
of death lowered into me, though I can't see any of it
until I see it in Rembrandt's scene, the doctor,

in his witches' hat, one hand clamping the tendons,
his other training its shadow on the wall as the dead
man reaches through the puppet-sock of the doctor's

robes to take control, and Rembrandt, unblinking,
seemingly unchanged, works and waits for God's love
to come down, sharp and cruel as a spade which misses,

again, the swifter beast coiling back inside of him.

Renoir, Arthritic

He's up early, considering the body,
its wetness, the bladder
like a puffer fish, the bowels
swallowing and swallowing,
mucus, come, blood, the soft crab
of the heart, darkly breathing,
the lungs spread out in the chest
like wings of a manta-ray,
not to mention the rich coral
of brain, the whole body
a trapped sea, netted in the skin,
perception itself just the motion
of the waves, the boat-wake
of experience healing into memory,
so that lying there, waiting to ring
the tiny silver bell that brings the nurse,
he feels his arthritis like a drought
inside of him, knowing the curative waters
at Bourbonne are no good, no good
the medicinal drip, his hand bruised
this morning where the brush was
strapped to it, though perhaps a bit of cloth
might be used between his fingers
and the wood, so that he can
continue to paint, to become
his rose-filled models, to feel
the elasticity of them, their fluidity
even in the hard desert-turtle
of his hand, so that he can continue
staring through the three-pronged

compass of the easel, until he gives
the signal and the canvas is raised
before him, like a sail, and he begins
to work, leaning forward, squinting,
drifting towards the horizon that he makes.

Michelangelo's Seizure

When it happened, finally,
on the preparation bridge,
where he had stood all morning
grinding the pigments, grooming
his brush-tips to a fine point
so that he could thread Eve's hair
like a serpent down her back,
his head rocked forward on the bell-chain
of his spine, the catwalks
rattling as he fell, a paint-
bowl splattering the ceiling,
then spinning like a dying bird,
to the chapel floor, frightening
the assistant who—trained
in such matters—huffed up
the footbridge to wedge
the handle of a wooden brush
between the mouse-trap of the teeth,
to keep the master from biting off
his tongue. Did the choir-box
fill with angels? Did the master
feel the beast rising up in him
to devour the pearl of heaven
at the center of his brain? If you
were that assistant, kneeling
next to the stampeded body,
smelling the quicklime in the air,
the boiled milk of plaster, seeing him
tangled in the body's vines, voiceless,
strained, would you call it rapture?
The assistant didn't either, didn't even

consider it, or think to pray,
but sat watching as the spirit clattered
back inside of him, like a chandelier
lowered from a ceiling—
and when it was over, he thought
he heard the artist curse softly
as he surfaced, a small word, violent,
so that when the master walked outside
to get some air, the boy sat atop
the scaffolding, eating his orange
and letting the fruit peels fall,
like drips of flame, feeling freer
in a way, almost glad. Outside,
it was fall, the city proud
with chimneys. Ragged, clouds
of plaster in his beard, his mouth
hollow, aching like an empty purse,
Michelangelo could still hear
the tortured voices on the ceiling
calling out for completion,
amputated, each face shadowed
with his own, which he would paint,
one morning, with the witchcraft
hushed inside his veins,
onto the flayed skin of St.
Bartholomew, crumpled, fierce,
with two dead bugs crushed
into the paint, like that bit of terror,
he would think, sealed inside
of everything He makes. Now
he lifted his fingers to his lips,
to the wasp's nest of his mouth,
and withdrew, with the ease of spitting
out an apple stem, a tiny splinter
of wood that had sunk into his tongue.

Late Self-Portrait

after Rembrandt

Outside, the city suffocates, infected with death-carts,
    ash-heaps in the yards, beds
        burned or dumped in the canals,
      some stained, some with imprints sunk in, like canvases,
    he thinks, the whole history of art
swept forward on the current of our loss. Contemplative,
    cold, his vision stepping out
        to the balcony again, Rembrandt sees
nothing that he needs, and so retreats back
    into the castle of his inwardness. If the soul,

he thinks, is a stone dropped in the center of the face,
    the face sealed back over it, but wavering,
        changed, then this morning he must paint
more distantly, self-love abolished to the province
    of the weak, the mirror turned away from him,
the canvas laid out on a stretching board. The brush-tip
    reveals, beneath the splints of the initial lines,
        the eroding cliff-edge of his brow,
    the tumbles of hair almost statuary now, gray
      as chilled breath, each gesture unwrapping

the package of his face, the way he longs to unravel
    these loose bandages of age. For years now,
        watching himself aging in the paint,
he's felt the two ends of his life advancing towards
    each other with their lances drawn, a confrontation
that ends, always, with Saskia on the bed again, her body thinned
    to a field the horses of her illness ramble through,
        the smell of snake oil and vinegar
    in the room, the soiled sheets, her lungs shredded
      by the bloody cough that even now

he hears echo through the house. When she died,
　　he could not see, for days, through the dusting
　　　of his grief, until he revived a painting
　he had made of her, humble, unadorned,
　　and smothered her not in the sores that inhaled her
in her final days, but in a velvet skirt and furs,
　　peacock feathers in her hat, her drowned light
　　　resurrected into pearls, as if death
　were the ascension into royalty, or as if to make a gem
　　of her, something he could store in the jewelry box

of memory. Even now he needs just a glimpse
　　of it before he turns away—the dust, light-struck,
　　　catching in his throat—to crush
　the whole scene into the eyes, or so he can place a lock
　　of her in the middle of the canvas, rendered
in a penetrating, venomous light, a dab of death
　　in the orpiment, like light from a keyhole,
　　　as if he might look into her dying as he paints,
　like a boy who kneels before a door, mischievous,
　　full of wonder, until that other, colder self

drops the curtain of his face back over her again.

Part II

Caravaggio's *The Death of the Virgin*

Not humility, but the animal inside
that brought him here, the artist fugitive,
pensive beneath the rafters of a barn,
hiding out, his hands shamed with blood,
the future coming at him with a knife
as he plumps the hay together for a bed,
then kicks it astray, his interior lightning-
struck, made visible by the suddenness
of his crime, the blood-thrum and God's presence
hammering inside of him, the man's face
carved onto the tablet of his memory, Caravaggio
pacing, tearing at his shirt, wanting God
out of him, thinking, isn't that how the Virgin
felt, water-broke among the horse-stench,
the slop, pain thorning deeper in her side
with each heave, the child crowned,
Joseph dumb-struck, trembling, one hand
ready at the blood-pail, one hand turning
the shoulders, trying to unscrew the child
from his mother's heart, though Mary
only thought *out, I need it out,* and the animals
around them lie down in the straw, already
hungry for the after-birth. But it's her death-
scene that unveils itself inside of him now,
Caravaggio feeling the images encircling
his heart, the way men close around a fight,
the eyes floated out across the surface of her face,
the body pale, breached, something glittering
swifted off in a confusion of wings, though she
must be in red, he thinks, the sun setting in her
dress, the Apostles astonished by its crimson

folds, their faces darkened by the shadow
of the savior's hand, the master turning them
away from the body, from his first temptation,
the nipple that ripened in the child's mouth,
deep and red as the inside of a plum,
the infant desire flaring into blood-lust
when the breast was pulled away, like the fury
we feel when love's withdrawn, which is why
he killed him, Ranuccio, his once-lover, the artist
pinning a corsage of blood onto his chest,
Ranuccio falling, stung, reaching dumbly
for his breast, like the gesture Caravaggio
will give the Virgin's hand when his canvases
are brought to him, as if she were buttoning
her dress, because she was also the first to tell
the child *no,* wasn't she? The first to deny him.

Magritte in New York

I hate my own history.
　—MAGRITTE

Looking out upon the hushed
　　　glass towers, the catwalks
　　and metal spires, the top
　　　of the Empire State Building,
　like the spike on a soldier's hat,
the whole city, he thinks, built
　　by an imagination more savage
　　　than he'd guessed, Magritte sees his own
　　mother lit up beneath the candelabra
of the Brooklyn Bridge, lifting her nightgown
　　　up above her knees to mount
　　the moon-slick railing, the night behind her,
　　　clotted with the traffic
　of the stars. He can see her slippered
footprints winding out behind her
　　　like the punctured roll of music
　　a player piano eats into song,
　　so that he can almost hear
　a singing as she falls, foghorns
in the distance, gulls startled from the girders
　　　when her gown peels up
　　around her, like an umbrella opened inside-
　　　out, like a woman lowered
　　through a cabaret, which is how they found her
on the shore that night, more than forty years
　　　ago, her head bound inside
　　　the nightgown.
He can still hear the lantern
　　　creaking in his father's hand,
　　can still see the light passed

across the water-toughened nipples,
        the glistening hair, the cleft
    between her legs. He couldn't help
but think of her kissing him
        again, how once he'd felt
    her tongue, soft and pink,
            like a bird hatched open
    in the nest of his mouth.
He had never seen a naked body before
        and even now, remembering it,
            trying to see through the fabric to
                the face,
    a darker image curdles up
        in him: two lovers,
entwined, a bed sheet wound between their heads.
    Is this how inspiration works,
he thinks, one image corrupted by the next?
        Tonight, looking out at the radio
    towers, at the ice-bergs of cathedral spires,
            he can't stop drawing,
    from an imagination
more savage than we'd guess, the exact line
    of his mother's breast,
            the moon unwinding its turban
    across the waves, as his father leans down
            to check the wrist for life, his mother's arm turned
                over in his hand, like a water-snake twisting
            its belly towards the light.

Self-Portrait as St. Sebastian Pierced by Arrows

after Egon Schiele

All form is under the anxiety
   of being looked at,
of being looked into,
   gaze after gaze rippling
through the body, like sound waves,
   until the entire body
is a listening, a scream called back
   in all directions
from its core. At home,
   watching Wally
in the stutters and twitches
   of sleep, I can mine,
without touching, a whimper
   out of her, then the flickering
of eyelids, like moths slowing
   themselves to land,
until I have teased
   her awake with my stare.
When we fuck,
   we are two mirrors
pressed together, each filled
   with the other's emptiness.
After, we sit and talk,
   and I watch the flaws
settle back into her face.
   Here, I am refused reflection,
refused color. Wally smuggles me
   pencils in her hair.
Mirror-less, unseen, I am fed
   straight out

into my perception, exiled
    into mop-handle
and rags, into cell door,
    my attention coiled
into bed springs,
    the frightening imbalance
of a chair. Down the hall,
    men sing to each other
across the rows, invisible,
    trying to melt the prison bars
with their singing, to charm
    the bars into snakes.
Each morning, in the murky,
    tadpole light
of an early dawn, we stand
    beneath the showers,
as if beneath halos, our pores
    opening, releasing
their steam, as if we might bind
    together in the air,
as if, floating among soap bubbles
    and groans, we might form
a collective deity. But objects
    keep commanding us—
spigots and drain holes erupting
    through the fog—
their presence echoing so deeply
    that their weight must be
what's holding us in place.
    I have taken the body
to the edge of collapse
    in exchange for my release.
I have translated the body
    into snarl, into deadfall
and crumb. I have prayed to be flayed,
    walking naked

through an eruption of bees,
    and I have woken
not to birdsong or the echoing
    of hobnails down the hall,
but to the sound of my own angelic
    twitching, the nerves
like a chorus of plucked strings,
    a quiver of quivering,
a hundred difficult muses
    launching their instructions
through the air. Even now, I wait
    for their arrows
to enter me, like pins into a voodoo
    doll, each pulled straight
through, so that it hauls a piece
    of flesh away—hunks
of fat, the meandering veins—
    their arrows made impotent
when my outline finally crumbles
    at their feet. Model
for my executioners, mirror-less,
    my shadow bricked
into the wall, I stand, body
    slack, abandoned
to its perpetual slouch, though
    one hand rises now,
palm open, like a handshake,
    or an offering.
Let them come for me,
    I think, *let them take*
the painting hand first.

The Death of Pointillism

after Seurat

Drought, gravel, broken glass, the houses
    in the distance like toppled carts
abandoned in the street, the channel
    narrowed to a wind-plucked hair,
to a broken guitar string shriveling beneath
    the song-less trees. No wind,
no rain, no motion in the scene, so that he must
    draw time, the shadowed quiet,
the weightless air (the greatest feat, Seurat
    once said, might be to make art
seem like work again), must break
    the landscape into seed, each kernel
pearled with light, like the globe
    Vermeer hung from a young girl's ear.
But how to re-assemble these crumbs
    back into wheat, how to heal
an evening sky grown ripe with stings,
    the mind working to un-mince, un-shred,
like trying to take back that shattering thing
    that can't be unsaid? Like light,
he thinks, lying is made of particles, words
    dropped or muffled with a cough,
so that he sees the channel narrow to a life
    he keeps trying to navigate—the wife
erased from speech, the un-willed son—
    until days from now, stricken,
his breath peeled back to a switch that beats
    and beats inside his chest, he bids
his parents to his bed to stand next to them,
    the four of them like directions

on a compass, each face a distant port,
    so that he understands there is no reaching
them, that like a choir rising, at its end,
    to a single voice, life is mended only
as it evaporates, the body swept up into a sandstorm,
    he imagines, scattered, then rebuilt
around its missing core, as if he might die
    exactly as he paints, with a shattering
that reforms the whole. Already, though,
    he feels his lies uncoiling inside
of him again, charmed from the basket
    of his body, his parents vanished,
his son God-knows-where, and a world away,
    his wife, at the sink, crying, snapping
peas, looking down into her hands,
    into the peeled-back husks and at
all the withered globes torn open to the light.

Vanitas for Robert Mapplethorpe
(1946–1988)

I.

He wanted only to live long enough to see the fame,
    and for years he was God of the rhino whips
and studs, God of the anus, cinched like the top of a purse,
        of the well-timed press release,
gossip carved by the knife-edge of his tongue,

the whole muscled world lounging in the perfume of his gaze,
    the open mouth of his camera lens inhaling
every pose, until he had captured them: the chiseled,
        the gorgeous, the famously ornery.
Now the fear grows out of him, the way a boy's dark hair

falls over his face, so that he's blinded by it,
    so that even when he sleeps
with a light on in his room, he thinks his own breath
        might extinguish it, his lungs fire-cleaned
and drained, AZT patrolling in his veins, his spine

a whipping post to which the tortured body clings,
    though, for the press, his body is the mess
at a party's end, the buffet wrecked by a hundred passing
        appetites, the magazines reporting AIDS
as if it were a fashion trend, he thinks,

though having the clippings read to him, each morning,
    he understands more deeply that dying *is* his fame,
doctors and flowers always on the way, the heart monitor's coverage
        around the clock, loved ones, fans,
the spotlights of their prayers, all of them breathless

as they wait for his soul to step out from behind the stage,
    as if it might shine above him when he dies,
like his own marquee.

2.

        Or, he knows, some hoping
        it might come out stained, black
as a furnace door, or the slip-card that concealed

the cover of the magazine he stole, sixteen
    and too ashamed to pay, the blind man
behind the counter chasing him for months inside his dreams,
        calling *Thief! Stop that little fag!* In hell,
his mother said, there was a clock that chimed each hour,

you will not get out, you will not get out, though yesterday,
    hobbled by a coughing fit, blacking out,
he felt his body folded into a paper boat and released
        across a stream. What happens
to all the undeveloped film inside the mind,

to the boxed-up wardrobe of our fantasies, he thinks,
    as he lies with a sketchpad flopped across
his lap, bed-sore, uninspired, one eye blind,
        the other weak, numbly scribbling
the knotted tie of his signature a hundred times,

"his final odd piece of ego and pornography," they'll say,
    "a ball of yarn unrolled from the center
of a narcissistic mind," though he sees it as that thicket
        of tangled selves we leave behind
when the soul has picked the body's locks,

his own body now like a photograph
    torn up in rage, so that everything left behind,
he thinks—memory, art—is left in pieces, like shells
    abandoned when the tide withdraws,
though already another tide, muscular, enormous,

moves inside the muted room with starlight
    curled inside its breaks, so that he feels not scared,
but awe-struck, dwarfed, like a small boy hurrying
    to scrawl his name into the sand
before it is erased by the censoring waves.

Jackson Pollock Driving

Mile by mile, the road unwinds backwards
through his mind, until he feels the whole system
    of highways and interstates inside of him,
masculine, instinctive, its form constructed
        to let the motion through, though lately,
    beneath each line, the underpass

of his second thoughts unfurls, doubt eating away
        at each canvas, like grub worms
        beneath a field, so that he's drawn
            into the spread roots of the painting
that isn't being born, his instinct fracturing,
    like spidered glass, until he's nearly overcome

    with the desire to let the paint can drop, boot-prints
wandering the frame, or something subtler,
        a few lingering brush-flicks, olive-drops
of color splitting open on the vines,
        as if even his failure could be his own,
    which may be how he'd feel, he thinks, if his tires

angled from the road, the asphalt curling off behind him,
        like a whip swung at him and missed,
    the car turned over, its beautiful underside
        of struts and muffler pipes glinting
    in the light. Does it have to be like that now, he thinks,
amputating, swift, the roulette ball of our random lives

dropped into the basket on some universal wheel?
Or can its motion be reversed? Raging,
    baffled by the critics, he'd held
    a knife up to a canvas and shouted, "you ought
to be able to slice a painting open like a chest."
    And what would he have found?

Veins? An orchard grove? Some other tangled life,
    like the one sliding out beneath him
    as he drives, a woman's head on his shoulder, the oil-
drippings of her hair spilled across his shirt, knotted,
    intricate, random as skate-marks
    on a frozen lake, the road polished to mirage,

    as if he could dive into it, he thinks,
the pond of what-he-might-have-been,
    that other world, where he turns, no,
    doesn't turn the wheel, and the radio turns to static,
and the road keeps winding out before him like a wick.

Francis Bacon in His Studio

1.

Like a man sitting inside his own decay,
the mine-walls of decorum chipped away

by the chisel of his inwardness: cartons
and rags, the snake-skins of a thousand

empty paint tubes among a garden
of brushes, mixing tins, toppled cans,

cigarette butts, wrappers, every interior
exhausted, except his own, which breaks all form

open to search for the seed of itself,
as if it were a con-game, the jewel

passed from shell to shell, while the dumbstruck
artist searches the rubble for the one lost crumb

that can solve the surface, the one that dropped
when the flap of skin fell open on his face.

2.

Long before the flap of skin peeled back like a corn-
husk, he thought, *how odd it is to have been born*

with a face at all. He kept imagining its imprint
in his mother's womb, solidified there, like hand-prints

in concrete, though his real face kept changing,
like the surface of a lake, carved by stress, aging,

the lightning-quick switch-blades of other people's
glances, so that each morning he had to sweep

away the old face with a lather brush and splash
a new one on when he had finished. Not a mask

exactly, but like wearing a weather-map, or the face
of a clock, which isn't worn, but drawn and erased

and redrawn by the erratic light inside a room,
so that he felt like a character from some cartoon,

caught inside those claustrophobic boxes, like panels
of a triptych. Always the face wobbled, like Cezanne's

fruit, so that he kept having to adjust himself to fit
behind it, as if he were trying to get comfortable

inside a strait-jacket, squirming, his face turning
around him like a globe, as the soul tried to worm

to the surface, to wriggle through the coils and twists
of thought and eat the light before it was extinguished

in the cells. Working one night, a fissure perforated one side
of his face, the web loosening around the spider of an eye

until that flap of skin slouched forward, like a woman fainting,
that dramatically, and his darkness spilled into the painting.

Part III

The Burning of Parliament, 1834

after J. M. W. Turner

He can see the flames settled deep in their faces,
    that reflective urge he's noticed lately in the skin,
all the onlookers hypnotized,
        tipsy in the half-shells of their boats,
    some praying, some clasping jugs of wine,
as they turn towards Parliament, rooting themselves

into the mud, the strangled chain of each anchor turning
    spinal underneath, like the smoke that unknots
continually above, almost umbilical,
        though it anchors the sky to the dead,
    the consumptive, industrious smoke, marbled
with ashes and grains of exploded glass, on its way to convert

the screams of the dying into rain. Walking out along the dock-
    boards of his vision, a glob of yellow
on his palette, like a coin
        he dips into with his brush,
    as if the whole color might be spent
on the extravagance of flames, Turner feels the fire

become a small glow that fills him as he paints,
    like a secret growing in importance,
as if, when he lets it back out
        into the landscape,
    it might restore the holy mystery, might end
the authority of shape. Palette knife, mineral spirits dissolving

in a solvent cup, umbrella pluming from the mud,
   each brushstroke is a flamboyant wound, the way,
in his father's barber-shop,
      for the first time being shaved,
   among water froth and steam, the gleaming metal,
soap stirred onto a lather brush, the scissors chirping like a beak,

he felt, as punishment for some forgotten sin, his father
   twitch his wrist, just slightly, to make
a nick into his skin,
      the crushed petals of his blood
   darkening a cloth, the moment already clotted
in his face. Though now, as his father's gesture renews itself

as paint, as epileptic flinches on the canvas,
   each motion quick as flipping a watch lid
closed, the past awakens
      into candle-dust and hue,
   a match-stroke grown into the flickering landscape,
so that, standing there, with the wind-caught flames slurred

above the bay, he begins to see the present as a shore
   from which to watch the past disintegrate,
the way, bored, he traced
      his outline onto the steam-
   fogged window of his father's shop,
then let the cold leak in, and breathless, watched himself

evaporate, his ghost-self trapped in the suffocating
   glass, as he imagined being tossed
through the window
      of his own body, the body
   shattering behind him. And doesn't
freedom, at last, have to be like that—fracturing, bold—

the self a border we cross and cross into flames, which,
       even now, are less a destruction
than the eviction of what lay,
         for years, ripening within,
       each board erupting with the sizzle passed
down through the wick of his veins, the coin-glint

from Parliament's chambers swirled into the paint,
       as if its arguments and pleas, the deep red
gloves pulled on
           by the executioning judge
       could be sewn together in the blaze. Once,
with sleight of hand, his father polished a coin into a cloth,

then tossed the bankrupt fabric in the air, as if the money
       might lay vaulted in the steam, though
at the time, confused,
           awe-struck in his father's light,
       he felt as if the coin might be locked
in him, hard and inextinguishable, radiating beneath

the skin, erupting, like the spirit, through the pores,
       though later, sweeping—now the image
slides out behind the paint,
           as Parliament collapses
       in a heap—he found the coin, still
smoldering, beneath the mound of a day's forsaken hair.

The Raft of the Medusa

after Theodore Gericault

It's like standing all day on a trapdoor, the anticipation
    worse than whatever waits below, the raft
rigged beneath their feet, cursed, their ship decomposing
    on some tribal shore, and the life-boats,
where finer men eat with knife and plate, unburdened

when the captain, maddened by his crew's slow pace,
    cuts the tow-ropes, as if to drop the curtain
on this make-shift stage, the frayed-rope ends sinking
    in the waves, a birth-cry rising from the planks
as the deserted men watch their noble brothers float away

on loaves of bread, already eyeing the water-jugs, the diminishing
    shoreline of each man's chest, the water
saying *what have you done, what have you done* as it crests
    across their feet, the horizon taking down the sail
each wave-tip makes. And what *have* they done? The sharks

of paranoia circling the crumb of each man's faith,
    the sail ragged as their bodies on its wooden
spine, and a trail of corpses left behind, like campfires
    abandoned on the forest floor, burnt-out,
some men slipping off the edge, a few throats slashed

in the middle of the night, their clothes ripped off
    and waved, not like rescue flags,
but like handkerchiefs thrown down at the beginning
    of a fight, death the admission that must be paid
for each new day, the flesh used, at first, for bait,

until the saliva triggers in the glands, and each corpse
    becomes a suitcase that's been rifled through.
Like a lid removed from a pot of stew, Gericault thinks,
    years later, toxins steaming up when the skin
is peeled away, the body laid out in the basement of the morgue,

where he's come to copy death in a plague of lines,
    the canvas still half-finished, adrift somewhere on
his cottage floor because, though he's seen the arm-muscles
    made thin at death, like strips of wax, felt the teeth
ground down to nubs of chalk, he can't quite finish it.

He's brushed the bodies together on the canvas, like a stack
    of leaves, aimed the arrowhead of the sail away
from them, so that the viewer must feel the desperation
    of their reach, only the dead looking out,
save one man that he's cloaked in an aura, a crust of red,

who wanders the sea-bottom of his own ravaged mind.
    Still, there's something unfinished in the scene,
something not quite said, until, later, in his uncle's
    bed, floating on the buoyancy of hips, he
and his aunt rowing towards completion, her body

splashing up through the bottom of his own, he looks
    down into the smoke and oil of her eyes
and feels something like a mutiny rise up inside
    of him, so that he understands he really
could leave his uncle weeping on the floor, overthrown,

though, all at once, he feels marooned when he has come,
    his aunt turning away from him again,
dressing quickly, sighing, "What have we done?"
    so that watching her smooth the covers
with her palm, the canvas remakes itself inside of him again,

the scene shaded now with all the broken oaths of France,
    lives cut off by the velocity of guillotines,
the constitution unrolled like a carpet for the King
    to walk across on his way back to the throne.
He will make them see the sail as a royal crest about to fall

from the edge of their gaze, a tortured flag twisted
    in the hand of the final healthy man, the bodies below,
monumental, cold, all he has to stand upon, which is how he feels
    as he's ghosted from his uncle's home, defiant,
mean, on his way to build, from this suffering, a new regime.

The Death of Sardanapalus

I have seen the death mask of my poor Gericault! To die among all one has created, in all the passion and vigor of youth.
—EUGENE DELACROIX

Operatic, bold, the sultan laid out in his ghostly robes,
    all ruined luxury, opium-faced, reposed,
the whole scene, candlestick and drapery, about to be torched,
    the Kingdom spilling its jewels at his feet.
Here is suicide made opulent, harem-girls rubbing oil

into their skin to make their corpses gleam, sword-
    blades singing through the horses' throats,
a slaughterhouse concerto, and Delacroix, frenzied
    as a conductor beneath his dark symphony
of hair, trying to paint the motion in, as if one cymbal-

crash of inspiration might ignite the scene, the horse-
    blood, ashes, drops of poison in the wine,
the rebels just outside the door, the sultan thinking, *let them
    conquer nothing, the pearl-dust
of a vanished history,* though it's France he paints, of course,

playing the sheet-music of its past on a foreign instrument,
    an elegy for the cities Napoleon plundered
in retreat, plucking what he could from the grape-
    bunch of each city's gems, the rest left to shrivel
beneath the bee-storm of a blaze, or the monarchy restored,

like a slow internal bleeding, though to love the self,
    Delacroix thinks, is to love our ruined history,
the shadow of his country's borders collapsing in his veins,
    the way, at death, the edges of the body flee,
so that it's Gericault he calls into the scene, horse-thrown,

capsized, his body being swallowed by the dust-storm
    of its own retreat, each breath like a nail yanked
from wood, and his paintings, those bent and mournful faces
    he made of the insane, arranged about the bed,
as pallbearers, Delacroix thought, the master having sealed

himself into the asylum of each frame. Ragged, obedient,
    feeding twigs of Gericault into the furnace
of the sultan's face, Delacroix feels the master taking
    hold of him as he paints, the way in a lesson
he'd latch onto a wrist, the ego heeled when the master

tightened the collar of his grip, as if to paint as someone
    else was to paint blameless, unconstrained,
like soldiers touched by the King's spirit as they fight,
    though it's just another romance, isn't it,
like Gericault thinking heaven lay scattered in the paint,

or believing the sultan, robe-swaddled, wrapped
    in the darkening clouds of his defeat,
condemning and condemned, feels each wound
    open in him a corresponding scream,
while his most faithful servants, open-mouthed, insane,

swallow jewels wrapped in cubes of bread, thinking
    they'll smuggle a piece of the master's soul
with them to their grave. Don't they know,
    by now, that no earthly thing—not mercy,
skin or oil—will stop the invasion of the blades?

Goya at the Madhouse

So this is where a love of the imagination leads,
    Goya thinks, boarded-up inside his deafness,
quarantined, silence inside of him like embalming fluid,
    the whole scene swirling around him as he draws,
as if he's come here to watch a storm from the quietest

of rooms, to feel each scream wash up
    against him and retreat, men grappling
with each other, some naked, some muddied with
    their shit, one man hung in chains, one eating
his shadow off another's back, though most wander

through the mine-shafts of their interiors, oblivious
    to the rubble of the others, curled up or sifting
through the hourglass of sleep. So this is where it leads,
    the hieroglyphic mind, the grapeshot
of our fantasies ignited in the groin: self-pollution,

widow's mites, leprosy. Last month, fevered, chattering,
    the dust-gnats of infection devouring
the petals in each ear, he saw, above him,
    a ceiling hung with snakes, constellations
in his bed fleece, lice in the dark hair of the night,

the doctor drawing a vial of ashes from his wrist,
    so that he felt himself disappearing,
as if he were being devoured by the larva
    in the doctor's eyes, by the madness
rising through the infinity of roots the mind unrolls

through the flesh's darkest soils, madness carving
    its way up the totem of the spine,
prehistoric, raw, from the body's Godless aquifers,
    until he began to see thought
as the salt the body's stormy ocean twirls weightless

through the air, our chain-linked logic unable
    to keep caged the animal of our history,
each revolution giving rise to the bloody code,
    the Inquisition, the guillotine.
So this is where it leads, starvation, dunking tubs

and whirling chains, the attendant in the corner with
    a lashing stick, our reason the mortar
with which authority lays its bricks, these men
    the windfall apples of their age
or strapped, from birth, into the wheelchairs of their destinies.

So this is where a lifetime of painting leads, staring up
    all day into the rotunda of the mind,
drawing now one man with a paper crown, one quailed
    beneath the soft beak of a Hussar's cap,
trying to suggest a balance in the filth, as if the inmates

were working towards a common goal, like shipbuilders,
    as if the madhouse might rise
on a battlement of shrieks, each inmate walking
    the gangplank of his sanity, he thinks,
like the time, as a boy, he found himself trapped

atop the catwalk in a barn, sealed inside the asylum
    stench of straw and pigeon shit,
the ladder dropped below, the dark complete,
    until, creeping forward, he popped
the hay-loft window and looked upon a landscape

he could not reach, the crops fenced in by stone,
    the farmhouse too distant for his screams,
which is how he felt when his madness finally broke,
    lofted, alone, waiting for art to let down its ropes
and lower him back into the flattened world below.

Double Elegy, 1918

1. Edith Schiele on Her Deathbed

Flickering, erased, her face claims him
as it defeats itself, the citrus cheeks,
windsock of her pony-tail,

though he sees this only inwardly,
in his reversible gaze. The rag of the real
face, lacquered, medicinal,

might be lifted away, might be wrung
out in the sink, as the soul might be twisted
from the body as she squirms

in a claustrophobic sleep, the sheets
soaked in ice-water, a heat in her
that could sizzle grease, the tugboat

of each cough dragging up a bit
of lung, the fetus dead or dying,
the radiant spill of cells starting

to poison it, the ember of each cell
darkening as it falls, the snake-
skin of the umbilicus closing down.

The sun, like a curled fox, unwinds
into dawn outside the window,
and Schiele tries only to sketch her

as she fades, to see how few lines
he can draw her in. If he could share
the thinning fact of her, like an ice-

cube passed between their mouths
during sex, he could recreate her dying
when she's gone, the pages flipped forward

so all that's left is the fossil of a cheekbone,
or the bottom lip, like a last splash of liquor
rimmed inside a glass, and then less than that—

the dark crumb of a mole, the eye's
packed ash, some irreducible flake of her,
like the one infected cell, just now,

he inherits from her breath.

2. The Death of Egon Schiele

Three days later, that cell like a shout
    that calls the rebels
from the woods, like a mis-struck note
    that pollutes a song,
or the first drop of rain upon a shoulder,
    has turned his body
to mudslide, to oil-spill, a disaster
    that finds no town near
and so destroys itself, like the shot
    that killed the Arch-Duke,
Schiele thinks, though what's inside
    of him, he knows,
was fired straight from the rifle
    of his Edith's mouth,
the infection like a drop of poison
    in him now, slithering,
expanded into memory, the gasoline
    fumes of his breath,
as the bed begins to take him in,
    an unrolling of muscles
and roots, as if he were trying to embrace
    Edith below, death
a loneliness that won't be resolved,
    or as if he were shoveling
trenches again, uniformed, sweating,
    blind in a forest
of spade-handles, fatigues, curses,
    weeks without knowing
where Edith was, or with whom,
    as he doesn't know now,
a thought that crawls through him,
    as all his thoughts crawl
down the ladder of themselves
    and other thoughts come

to spill the earth back over them,
    though it's him they're digging
into it, isn't it, his body a stretch of dirt
    that must be cleared
away, the men circled above,
    their faces all cigarettes
and mud, the shells launched
    above their heads leaving
tracings in the air. "Mother, I need
    the oxygen!" he calls,
and the black-hearted spades
    keep erasing the weakening earth.

The Machine Gunner's Letters

(as Otto Dix)

I.

How, you write, will I survive? With instinct, trigger-eye,
the soldiers like turtles flipped over in the mud, limb-flail
and broken shell. These thoughts move through me as I write,
a telegraph tape slipping through fingers. The lumberjack,
they call me, timber in the field, green blemished by red-splatter,
like leaves at fall's beginning. Behind the gun, I am eternity,
I am time looking out from the inside of a clock, the click-
stop finger that marks the finish line. My body, knuckle-ache
and recoil, records each loss, tally-marks on the black slate
of the heart. I am the vomit-taste in the mouth, what they know
is watching, though they race towards me as I hand death out,
a parade-master tossing candy to the crowd. Later, under star-
flutter, the night opening parachutes as it falls, I have to pick,
like needles from a pin-cushion, the splintered death out of me.
How once, I made your body gleam, the tongued lips, boot-
polish on the nipples, your skin rubbed with orange peels.
I could have, then, painted beautifully. Now, even the most
gentle touch dissolves, my finger harp-strumming the trigger,
grenade pin held between the teeth. Love, all night the gun,
cartridge oil, rivet, barrel clip, puts itself together in my mind.
It's so quiet out there, I can almost hear the maggots trash-
picking the fields, or the final woman-call a body makes.
Someone should rat-skitter through the foxholes, the moon-
stricken thistle-bush, and close their awful, glowing mouths.
Someone, mercy-handed, should sew this trench-line closed.

2.

Shell-glow, tracer flare, shock troops huddled in a dawn field
affixing their masks. These glints of beauty, aren't they just
the gilded edge of the sword, a muffle for the cruelty? Mother,
I've seen boys with bat-poison in their veins, rabid, climbing
the trench walls to let themselves be shot, have seen the recruits,
target-faced, naive, linger on the fire-step, their heads bobbed
above the parapet, like trench-line puppeteers. I have pearled
the bullet deep into the broken oyster of each face. Last night,
a hole opened in me and closed. I dream-walked the fields,
unharmed, healing shell-holes with a touch, the seed-bag
of my body slowly tearing open as I walked. When I woke, rats
at my boot-leather, the moon with its machete at my throat,
I could hear the shrapnel sing, could hear the instruments of war
play themselves inside of me, the whole trench an orchestra pit
where I conducted the music of the gun, each snap-trigger
note moving backwards through my hand, until my body was
the absence of a song, a white-nothing firing at the advancing
troop-line of the dawn, at the field-breath, at the mist, the building
sea-wall of the dead, all chest wounds and buckle glint, bayonets
of sunlight breaking through the fog. I remember the kitchen-
light, bathwater boiling on the stove, you lice-picking my hair,
fingernail and turpentine, dropping them into the lantern flame,
hovering above me with bible-verses in your voice, the curse
of rodents, locust-plagues, telling me we are, each of us, earth-
sky divided in the veins, death a way to sort the filthy from
the clean. Fingernail, turpentine, who will pick these memories
out of me? The corpse-light rising from the fields, the nail-hole
of each nerve opening as I up-tilt the gun, like a conductor marking
the crescendo of a song, my aim noses skyward, as if to kill
the emptiness I know is there, the emptiness that rots inside
of everything, inside our ration packs, the quick-lime, inside
the ripening grenades, inside the shit-fumes that smoke the air,
inside the burnt-out sockets of the gassed, the beehives of their lungs,
inside the canteens of our hearts, inside the boot-water rats,

the maggots that punctuate each corpse, inside the dead laid out
all night upon the field, open-mouthed, code-breakers baffled
by the language of stars, inside these words, inside everything I
paint, inside the quick-saluting boy I death-slouched against
the parapet, the dog-tags torn from his throat, inside the spirit
of the boy, mother-trained, following orders even as he dies,
a hand held up at the exit of himself, then waving him through,
waving him into kitchen light, bathwater boiling on the stove,
where you first told me of the polished soul, where, as if to
demonstrate the violence with which it enters us, you pressed
a fingernail sharp against my cheek, shining, bullet-tipped.

Gassed

after John Singer Sargent

They might as well be walking towards a firing squad, blind-
folded, single-file, a guide wire strung between them, each man
a wounded Theseus crawling back up from the underworld,

though this thread leads only to the infirmary, where the gas
will shut their bodies down, will move between the bodies' rooms
and snuff each lantern out. The dying grasp at their pant-legs

as they pass, as they wobble along the duckboards just above
the mud gasping at their feet, the steaming trash heaps
of the dead, the battlefield sloppy as a butcher's floor, all blood

and aftermath, the dusk-glint of God turning to put his knives
away. Looking out through the insect eyes of his mask,
fatigued, Sargent can't quite believe he's not imagined them,

called them up from the foxholes of a torched and rubbled mind,
a mind battered by three weeks at the front, burrowed into itself
and paranoid. At home, he worked slowly, sitting for days

with his models, spoonfuls of pigment tapped onto the scales,
working the empathetic muscles until he could roll the stone
of each face away. He painted through the nights when the black-

out curtains fell, Paris, light-starved and feverish with sirens,
the newsstands charred, the smoldering grill-pits of bombed-
out cars, the city blown back, in scraps, through his memory,

so that even now when a flock of poisoned birds begins to fall,
one by one, into No Man's Land, like descending souls,
he sees them as cathedral stones, *Saint Gervais* collapsing

again with his niece inside, Sargent, astonished, absorbed,
but not quite there, brushing the air-borne plaster from his coat
like snow, watching the wheelbarrows teeter under the rubble-

weight, the stretchers hauling off the faithful dead, one man
mouthing, for eternity, a final hymnal note, and the girl's face
erased but everywhere, in the rag-pile of the church, reflected

in the cobblestone, his mind, in pain, unable to see her death
except in metaphor. Even here, where the bodies are given
a brief skeletal radiance in the shell light, as if he really might see

into them, he edits the horror out, no vomit, no severed limbs,
the faces a touch too bright, each man with his hand
on the shoulder of the one in front of him, like elephants

hooked snout to tail, the men washed and strung along
the line, as if he might make our soiled history clean again.
Or is it just another drop of poison stirred into the wine,

he thinks, a way to make the wretched tolerable? What else
could he do, an old man who knew by now this war
would be the end of him, who knew even if he could paint

the blistered, naked bodies, the shit streaking down the inside
of a man's thigh as he walks, the white angel-maggots burrowing
into a face, his mind, at its core, could not help making things

beautiful. With the night turning purple as the gas disperses
through the atmosphere, Sargent works with his mask slung
across his shoulder like an extra face, letting his inspiration

filter all doubts away as he sutures the men back together
with a pencil tip, as he feels them moving through his thoughts
like a line of text, written nearly a century later by a man

with a book of paintings open on his desk, who sits and watches
the rain fall into the empty flowerpots outside his window,
which he can't help seeing as the upturned helmets of the dead.

STEVE GEHRKE teaches creative writing at Seton Hall University. He is the author of *The Pyramids of Malpighi: Poems,* for which he won the Philip Levine Prize for Poetry, and *The Resurrection Machine,* for which he was awarded the John Ciardi Prize for Poetry. His poems have appeared in numerous journals, including the *Kenyon Review, Yale Review,* and *Slate.* For the poems in this book, he received a grant from the National Endowment for the Arts and a Pushcart Prize.

Illinois Poetry Series

Laurence Lieberman, Editor

The Ways We Touch
Miller Williams (1997)

The Rooster Mask
Henry Hart (1998)

The Trouble-Making Finch
Len Roberts (1998)

Grazing
Ira Sadoff (1998)

Turn Thanks
Lorna Goodison (1999)

Traveling Light:
Collected and New Poems
David Wagoner (1999)

Some Jazz a While:
Collected Poems
Miller Williams (1999)

The Iron City
John Bensko (2000)

Songlines in Michaeltree: New and
Collected Poems
Michael S. Harper (2000)

Pursuit of a Wound
Sydney Lea (2000)

The Pebble: Old and New Poems
Mairi MacInnes (2000)

Chance Ransom
Kevin Stein (2000)

House of Poured-Out Waters
Jane Mead (2001)

The Silent Singer: New and Selected
Poems
Len Roberts (2001)

The Salt Hour
J. P. White (2001)

Guide to the Blue Tongue
Virgil Suárez (2002)

The House of Song
David Wagoner (2002)

X =
Stephen Berg (2002)

Arts of a Cold Sun
G. E. Murray (2003)

Barter
Ira Sadoff (2003)

The Hollow Log Lounge
R. T. Smith (2003)

In the Black Window: New and
Selected Poems
Michael Van Walleghen (2004)

A Deed to the Light
Jeanne Murray Walker (2004)

Controlling the Silver
Lorna Goodison (2005)

Good Morning and Good Night
David Wagoner (2005)

American Ghost Roses
Kevin Stein (2005)

Battles and Lullabies
Richard Michelson (2005)

National Poetry Series

Eroding Witness
Nathaniel Mackey (1985)
Selected by Michael S. Harper

Palladium
Alice Fulton (1986)
Selected by Mark Strand

Cities in Motion
Sylvia Moss (1987)
Selected by Derek Walcott

The Hand of God and a Few
Bright Flowers
William Olsen (1988)
Selected by David Wagoner

The Great Bird of Love
Paul Zimmer (1989)
Selected by William Stafford

Stubborn
Roland Flint (1990)
Selected by Dave Smith

The Surface
Laura Mullen (1991)
Selected by C. K. Williams

The Dig
Lynn Emanuel (1992)
Selected by Gerald Stern

My Alexandria
Mark Doty (1993)
Selected by Philip Levine

The High Road to Taos
Martin Edmunds (1994)
Selected by Donald Hall

Theater of Animals
Samn Stockwell (1995)
Selected by Louise Glück

The Broken World
Marcus Cafagña (1996)
Selected by Yusef Komunyakaa

Nine Skies
A. V. Christie (1997)
Selected by Sandra McPherson

Lost Wax
Heather Ramsdell (1998)
Selected by James Tate

So Often the Pitcher Goes to Water
until It Breaks
Rigoberto González (1999)
Selected by Ai

Renunciation
Corey Marks (2000)
Selected by Philip Levine

Manderley
Rebecca Wolff (2001)
Selected by Robert Pinsky

Theory of Devolution
David Groff (2002)
Selected by Mark Doty

Rhythm and Booze
Julie Kane (2003)
Selected by Maxine Kumin

Shiva's Drum
Stephen Cramer (2004)
Selected by Grace Schulman

The Welcome
David Friedman (2005)
Selected by Stephen Dunn

Michelangelo's Seizure
Steve Gehrke (2006)
Selected by T. R. Hummer

Other Poetry Volumes

Local Men and *Domains*
James Whitehead (1987)

Her Soul beneath the Bone: Women's
Poetry on Breast Cancer
Edited by Leatrice Lifshitz (1988)

Days from a Dream Almanac
Dennis Tedlock (1990)

Working Classics: Poems on Industrial
Life
*Edited by Peter Oresick and Nicholas
Coles* (1990)

Hummers, Knucklers, and Slow
Curves: Contemporary Baseball Poems
Edited by Don Johnson (1991)

The Double Reckoning of Christopher
Columbus
Barbara Helfgott Hyett (1992)

Selected Poems
Jean Garrigue (1992)

New and Selected Poems, 1962–92
Laurence Lieberman (1993)

The Dig and *Hotel Fiesta*
Lynn Emanuel (1994)

For a Living: The Poetry of Work
*Edited by Nicholas Coles and Peter
Oresick* (1995)

The Tracks We Leave: Poems on En-
dangered Wildlife of North America
Barbara Helfgott Hyett (1996)

Peasants Wake for Fellini's *Casanova*
and Other Poems
*Andrea Zanzotto; edited and translated
by John P. Welle and Ruth Feldman;
drawings by Federico Fellini and Augusto
Murer* (1997)

Moon in a Mason Jar and *What My
Father Believed*
Robert Wrigley (1997)

The Wild Card: Selected Poems, Early
and Late
*Karl Shapiro; edited by Stanley Kunitz
and David Ignatow* (1998)

Turtle, Swan and *Bethlehem in Broad
Daylight*
Mark Doty (2000)

Illinois Voices: An Anthology of
Twentieth-Century Poetry
Edited by Kevin Stein and G. E. Murray
(2001)

On a Wing of the Sun
Jim Barnes (3-volume reissue, 2001)

Poems
*William Carlos Williams; introduction
by Virginia M. Wright-Peterson* (2002)

Creole Echoes: The Francophone
Poetry of Nineteenth-Century
Louisiana
*Translated by Norman R. Shapiro;
introduction and notes by M. Lynn Weiss*
(2003)

Poetry from *Sojourner:* A Feminist Anthology
Edited by Ruth Lepson with Lynne Yamaguchi; introduction by Mary Loeffelholz (2004)

Asian American Poetry: The Next Generation
Edited by Victoria M. Chang; foreword by Marilyn Chin (2004)

Papermill: Poems, 1927–35
Joseph Kalar; edited and with an Introduction by Ted Genoways (2005)

The University of Illinois Press
is a founding member of the
Association of American University Presses.

Composed in 11/14 Adobe Garamond
with Porcelain Script and Impact display
by Celia Shapland
for the University of Illinois Press
Designed by Dennis Roberts
Manufactured by Sheridan Books, Inc.

University of Illinois Press
1325 South Oak Street
Champaign, IL 61820-6903
www.press.uillinois.edu